Encounters with God

The REVELATION of
Jesus Christ

Encounters with God Study Guide Series

The Gospel of Matthew

The Gospel of Mark

The Gospel of Luke

The Gospel of John

The Book of Acts

The Book of Romans

The First Epistle of Paul the Apostle to the Corinthians

The Second Epistle of Paul the Apostle to the Corinthians

The Epistle of Paul the Apostle to the Galatians

The Epistle of Paul the Apostle to the Ephesians

The Epistle of Paul the Apostle to the Philippians

The Epistles of Paul the Apostle to the Colossians and Philemon

The First and Second Epistles of Paul the Apostle to the Thessalonians

The First and Second Epistles of Paul the Apostle to Timothy and Titus

The Epistle of Paul the Apostle to the Hebrews

The Epistle of James

The First and Second Epistles of Peter

The First, Second, and Third Epistles of John and Jude

The Revelation of Jesus Christ

Encounters with God

The REVELATION of Jesus Christ

THOMAS NELSON
Since 1798

NASHVILLE   DALLAS   MEXICO CITY   RIO DE JANEIRO

Copyright © 2008 by

Henry Blackaby, Th.M., D.D.
Richard Blackaby, M.Div., Ph.D.
Thomas Blackaby, M.Div., D.Min.
Melvin Blackaby, M.Div., Ph.D.
Norman Blackaby, M.Div., B.L., Ph.D.

All rights reserved. No portion of this book may be reproduced, stored in a retrieval system, or transmitted in any form or by any means—electronic, mechanical, photocopy, recording, scanning, or other—except for brief quotations in critical reviews or articles, without the prior written permission of the publisher.

Published in Nashville, Tennessee, by Thomas Nelson. Thomas Nelson is a registered trademark of Thomas Nelson, Inc.

Thomas Nelson, Inc. titles may be purchased in bulk for educational, business, fund-raising, or sales promotional use. For information, please e-mail SpecialMarkets@ThomasNelson.com.

All Scripture quotations are taken from THE NEW KING JAMES VERSION. © 1982 by Thomas Nelson, Inc. Used by permission. All rights reserved.

ISBN 978-1-4185-2656-6

Printed in the United States of America

08 09 10 11 12 RRD 6 5 4 3 2

CONTENTS

AN INTRODUCTION
TO THE REVELATION OF JESUS CHRIST

This study guide covers The Revelation of Jesus Christ. The book is named for its first word, *apokalupsis*, which means to "unveil, disclose, or reveal." It was written to encourage believers in the seven churches in an area we now know as Turkey. These churches were very likely the foremost churches under the organizational leadership of John the apostle. They were situated in something of a circular pattern geographically, and they may have served as centralized postal centers for a much larger geographical region. It is likely that the entire book of Revelation was circulated to all the churches in the Roman province of Asia.

Through the years many people have questioned when John wrote Revelation. Current scholarship tends toward the view that John wrote Revelation in segments that may have been smuggled vision by vision, small piece of parchment by small piece of parchment, off the island of Patmos where John was imprisoned by Caesar. A monastery on the isle of Patmos has been in existence since AD 104, and the monastery leadership contends that John was exiled to a cave on the small rock island of Patmos to die, but John outlived the Caesar who had imprisoned him. He returned to Ephesus to live for at least two years after his imprisonment. The leaders of the monastery also contend that the letters of John were written prior to John's coming to Patmos, Revelation was written during his stay there, and the Gospel of John was written after his return to Ephesus. The monastery, they say, was built as a *praise* response for the revealed truths given to John *about Jesus*, not as a *prayer* response related to a prediction of future events.

The book is highly symbolic and full of imagery that likely was far more readily deciphered by John's contemporaries than by readers today. Thus, John had no need to provide explanations or give clues for unlocking the mysteries of the various experiences he had, the things he saw in the Spirit, or the things he heard as part of the visions given to him. A number of approaches have been taken through the centuries for interpreting Revelation: the *preterist view*, in which the prophecies are seen as referring to events taking place in the Roman empire during the first century with the return of Christ understood as being the only outstanding event yet to occur; the *historical view*, in which John is believed to have outlined the overall course of history looking toward Christ's return; the *futurist view*, in which chapters 4 and beyond are understood to describe only events related to the last days before Christ's return; and the *idealist view*, in which the book is read as a series of symbolic and imaginative descriptions of God's ultimate triumph over all enemies with no direct parallel to historical events.

We can be certain of one thing: overall, the book describes a trend of up-surging evil, the triumphant victory of Christ over that evil, and the reward of all faithful believers.

The purpose of the book was to exalt Christ, to admonish the churches to keep their focus on Christ, and to anticipate the victory of Christ as King of Kings, Alpha and Omega, Mighty Warrior, the Victor over all His enemies.

Many people refer to the book as eschatology, the Greek word that literally means "study of the last." Eschatology is not merely a study of the end times but the historic completion of the revealed purposes of God. The book's core idea is not the horror that might precede or be associated with the "end" but, rather, the triumphant return of Christ Jesus who turns the end of this age into a glorious new beginning.

The book of Revelation has also been called apocalyptic literature. This literary form flourished during the last two centuries before Christ and the first century after Christ. An apocalypse is a revelation or unveiling made by an angel or other celestial being. The message is expressed in vivid and sometimes picturesque symbols. The apocalyptists were pessimistic about human efforts to overcome evil, even as they expressed conviction that God would intervene and forcibly destroy evil forces that oppressed His people.

Revelation differs from traditional apocalyptic literature in several ways. Apocalypses were usually written in the name of an illustrious figure of the past. John emphasized that *he* was writing what had been personally revealed to him (Rev. 1:1, 4, 9; 21:2; 22:8). John's apocalypse is optimistic. Although it portrays a massive struggle between good and evil, John was confident that a decisive victory was coming and that human beings could repent of their errors and participate fully in the victory at hand. He repeatedly referred to his writing as *prophecy*, not apocalypse (Rev. 1:3; 22:7, 10, 18, 19)

About the Author, John. Most scholars believe the author of Revelation was the apostle John, fisherman son of Zebedee, brother of James, and one of Jesus' twelve apostles. He was in the innermost circle of three apostles together with Peter and James. It was John who stood by Jesus during His trial and stayed at the foot of the cross to hear Jesus charge him to care for

Mary, His mother. John was one of the first two apostles at the empty tomb. John outlived all of the other apostles and proclaimed throughout his entire life that he found meaning in only one central truth: he was loved by Christ, who had died as the atoning sacrifice for him and had given him the assurance of eternal life. Revelation is perhaps something of a bookend to John's proclamation that "God so loved the world that He gave His only begotten Son, that whoever believes in Him should not perish but have everlasting life" (John 3:16). In Revelation we receive the assurance that God *will* reward those who love Him in return.

AN OVERVIEW OF OUR STUDY
OF THE REVELATION OF JESUS CHRIST

This study guide presents seven lessons drawn from The Revelation of Jesus Christ. It elaborates upon the commentary included in the *Blackaby Study Bible:*

Lesson #1: Christ in the Midst of His Church

Lesson #2: Counsel to the Churches in Ephesus and Pergamos

Lesson #3: Counsel to the Churches in Thyatira, Sardis, and Laodicea

Lesson #4: Affirmation of the Churches in Smyrna and Philadelphia

Lesson #5: Praise in the Throne Room of Heaven

Lesson #6: Victory over Satan and All God's Enemies

Lesson #7: Our Heavenly Home

Personal or Group Use. These lessons are offered for personal study and reflection or for small-group Bible study. The study questions asked may be answered by an individual reader or used as a foundation for group discussion. A segment titled "Notes to Leaders of Small Groups" is included at the back of this book to help those leading a group study of this material.

Before you embark on this study, we encourage you to read in full the statement in the *Blackaby Study Bible* titled "How to Study the Bible." Our contention is always that the Bible is unique among all literature. It is God's definitive word for humanity. The Bible is

• *inspired*—"God-breathed"

• *authoritative*—absolutely the final word on any spiritual matter

- *the plumb line of truth*—the standard against which all human activity and reasoning must be evaluated

The Bible is fascinating in that it has remarkable diversity but also remarkable unity. Its books were penned by a diverse assortment of authors representing a variety of languages and cultures, and it contains a number of literary forms. But the Bible's message from cover to cover is clear, consistent, and unified.

More than mere words on a page, the Bible is an encounter with God Himself. No book is more critical to your life. The very essence of the Bible is the Lord Himself.

The Holy Spirit speaks through the Bible. He also communicates during your time of prayer, in your life circumstances, and through the church. Read your Bible in an attitude of prayer, and allow the Holy Spirit to make you aware of God's activity in and through your personal life. Write down what you learn, meditate on it, and adjust your thoughts, attitudes, and behavior accordingly. Look for ways every day to apply the truth of God's Word to your circumstances and relationships. God is not random; He is orderly and intentional in the way He speaks to you.

Be encouraged—the Bible is *not* too difficult for the average person to understand if that person asks the Holy Spirit for help. (Furthermore, not even the most brilliant person can fully understand the Bible apart from the Holy Spirit's help!) God desires for you to know Him and to know His Word. Every person who reads the Bible can learn from it. The person who will receive *maximum* benefits from reading and studying the Bible, however, is the person who:

- *is born again* (John 3:3,5). Those who are born again and have received the gift of His Spirit have a distinct advantage in understanding the deeper truths of God's Word.

- *has a heart that desires to learn God's truth.* Your attitude greatly influences the outcome of Bible study. Resist the temptation to focus on what others have said about the Bible. Allow the Holy Spirit to guide you as you study God's Word for yourself.

- *has a heart that seeks to obey God.* The Holy Spirit teaches the most to those who desire to apply what they learn.

Begin your Bible study with prayer, asking the Holy Spirit to guide your thoughts and to impress upon you what is on God's heart. Then make plans to adjust your life immediately to obey the Lord fully.

As you read and study the Bible, your purpose is not to *create* meaning, but to *discover* the meaning of the text with the Holy Spirit's guidance. Ask yourself, "What did the author have in mind? How was this applied by those who first heard these words?" Especially in your study of Paul's letters, look for ways in which the truths can be applied directly to your personal, practical, daily Christian walk and to the life of your church.

At times you may find it helpful to consult other passages of the Bible (made available in the center columns in the *Blackaby Study Bible*), or the commentary that is in the margins of the *Blackaby Study Bible*.

Always keep in mind that Bible study is not primarily an exercise for acquiring information but an opportunity for transformation. Bible study is your opportunity to encounter God and to be changed in His presence. When God speaks to your heart, nothing remains the same. Jesus said, "He who has ears to hear, let him hear" (Matt. 13:9). Choose to have ears that desire to hear!

The B-A-S-I-Cs of Each Study in This Guide. Each lesson in this study guide has five segments, using the word BASIC as an acronym. The word BASIC does not allude to elementary or simple, but rather to foundational. These studies extend the concepts that are part of the *Blackaby Study Bible* commentary and are focused on key aspects of what it means to be a Christ-follower in today's world. The BASIC acronym stands for:

B = *Bible Focus.* This segment presents the central passage for the lesson and a general explanation that covers the central theme or concern.

A = *Application for Today.* This segment has a story or illustration related to current-day events with questions that link the Bible text to today's issues, problems, and concerns.

S = *Supplementary Scriptures to Consider.* In this segment other Bible verses related to the general theme of the lesson are explored.

I = *Introspection and Implications.* In this segment questions are asked that lead to deeper reflection about one's personal faith journey and life experiences.

C = *Communicating the Good News.* In this segment challenging questions point to ways the lesson's truth might be lived out and shared with others, whether to win the lost or build up the church.

LESSON #1

CHRIST IN THE MIDST OF HIS CHURCH

Alpha: first letter of the Greek alphabet; the beginning

Omega: last letter of the Greek alphabet; the ending

"Alpha and Omega" was a phrase equivalent to our saying, "from A to Z"—which means **all-encompassing**

B
Bible Focus

> *I, John, both your brother and companion in the tribulation and kingdom and patience of Jesus Christ, was on the island that is called Patmos for the word of God and for the testimony of Jesus Christ. I was in the Spirit on the Lord's Day, and I heard behind me a loud voice, as of a trumpet, saying, "I am the Alpha and the Omega, the First and the Last," and, "What you see, write in a book and send it to the seven churches which are in Asia: to Ephesus, to Smyrna, to Pergamos, to Thyatira, to Sardis, to Philadelphia, and to Laodicea."*
>
> *Then I turned to see the voice that spoke with me. And having turned I saw seven golden lampstands, and in the midst of the seven lampstands One like the Son of Man, clothed with a garment down to the feet and girded about the chest with a golden band. His head and hair were white like wool, as white as snow, and His eyes like a flame of fire; His feet were like fine brass, as if refined in a furnace, and His voice as the sound of many waters; He had in His right hand seven stars, out of His mouth went a sharp two-edged sword, and His countenance was like the sun shining in its strength. And when I saw Him, I fell at His feet as dead. But He laid His right hand on me, saying to me, "Do not be afraid; I am the First and the Last. I am He who lives, and was dead, and behold, I am alive forever. Amen. And I have the keys of Hades and of Death. Write the things which you have seen, and the things which are, and the things which will take place after this. The mystery of the seven stars which you saw in My right hand, and the seven golden lampstands: The seven stars are the angels of the seven churches, and the seven lampstands which you saw are the seven churches"* (Rev. 1:9–20).

There are many things in the book of Revelation that cannot be readily understood or interpreted. We are going to focus on what *can* be readily understood, and the first of those truths is this: Jesus governs His church—the church throughout the ages, around the world, in all cultures and nations—which is His Body. Jesus stands in the midst of His people at all times, governing the churches and holding their leaders as a precious possession in His hands.

The foremost figure in the book of Revelation is Christ Jesus. In the opening chapter, He is pictured as having:

- head and hair white as snow (1:14)

- eyes like a flame of fire (1:14)

- feet like fine brass (1:15)

- voice loud as of a trumpet; voice as the sound of many waters (1:10,15)

- countenance like the sun shining in its strength (1:16)

- full-length clothing (1:13)

- a golden band girding his chest (1:13)

Each of these descriptive words and phrases is a well-known Jewish metaphor for tremendous power and authority. The Lord is radiant in his splendor and majesty. Elsewhere in Revelation, Jesus is described as:

- the Beginning of the creation of God (3:14)

- the faithful witness (1:5)

- the firstborn from the dead, the one who was dead and came to life (1:5; 2:8)

- the ruler over the kings of the earth (1:5)

- Alpha and Omega, the Beginning and the End, the First and the Last (1:8, 2:8, 22:13)

- the Faithful and True Witness (3:14)

- the Root and the Offspring of David (22:16)

- the Lion of the tribe of Judah (5:5)

- the Root of David (5:5)

- The Lamb (5:8)

- One like the Son of Man (14:14)

- the Bright and Morning Star (22:16)

Perhaps the greatest lesson we can ever learn from the book of Revelation is related to the identity of Christ Jesus. The more we know Jesus—the more we understand Who He is, why He came to earth, and how He reigns throughout eternity. The better we know Jesus, the more we have a desire to praise Him, worship and serve Him, and exalt Him as being the *only* One worthy of highest honor and glory. If you desire to know the Lord better, engage in your own study of the many attribute names ascribed to God the Father, God the Son, and God the Holy Spirit throughout the Bible.

In the opening statements of Revelation we also find these behavioral and character traits associated with the Lord:

- He holds seven stars in His right hand (1:16)

- He has a sharp two-edged sword proceeding from His mouth when He speaks (1:16), meaning that He speaks words that have the power of life and death

- He stands in the midst of seven lampstands (1:12)

- He embodies the seven spirits of God (3:1), or, He is fully God

- He is holy and true (3:7)

- He has the key prophesied by Isaiah: what He opens no one can close, and what he closes no one can open (3:7)

- He is Amen—which means "so be it." What He says *will* come to pass (3:14)

This set of descriptive terms is applied directly to the church. John sent a strong word, saying in essence, "Make no doubt about it, Jesus is in charge." He was, is, and always will be in charge of His Body. He holds not only the keys to the church but also the keys related to death and hell.

This message must have been tremendously comforting to the churches when they heard first heard it. Their "leader" had been imprisoned by Rome and was banished to Patmos to die. John declared, "Your *real* leader is very much alive and in charge, not only of the time of my death but of death itself."

Furthermore, John said, he saw the leaders of the seven churches in Jesus' right hand, the hand of authority and power. The leaders were presented as stars, a fixed and lasting witness, in contrast to the "wandering stars," a phrase used in the early church to describe false teachers. In John's vision, Jesus was standing at the center of a circle of seven lampstands, which John said were the seven churches of Asia Minor. Those who comprised these churches must have wondered what would happen to their leaders and their churches in the wake of John's imprisonment. John declared to them, "You are in Jesus' hands and He is in your midst."

The other New Testament books tell us about who Jesus as He lived out His ministry on this earth. Revelation tells us who Jesus is in heaven. It also tells us who *we* are in Christ.

No matter how we may feel individually or as churches, Jesus has not abandoned His Body. He holds us close to Himself. He stands in the midst of who we are. He commands what will happen and is ultimately in charge of what is accomplished.

What good news this is!

How would you *describe* Jesus to someone who had never heard about Him?

Do you firmly believe that Jesus is fully in charge of *you* as a Christian, and fully in charge of what happens in *your* church? What happens to a person or body of believers when they lift Jesus up in the fullness of His identity and acknowledge Him as the leader who is in control?

A
Application for Today

Dad came home to find three of his children playing with a group of neighborhood children in the backyard. In the corner of the yard sat their chocolate Labrador, Jack, with a red-white-and-blue scarf around his neck. He was "staying" where he had been commanded to stay. Some of the children were wearing bits of blue—bandanas, shirts, caps. Others were wearing bits of red.

"What's going on?" Dad asked Mom, who was watching the children from the shelter of a covered patio.

"Listen," said Mom.

The children in blue approached the children in red cautiously, as if they were new to the backyard and unsure of their surroundings. The children in red were obviously taking the role of permanent residents going about their usual duties in life.

Suddenly the children in blue took on a warrior stance, pulling out sticks and even the water hose to assert power. The children in red were suddenly the ones who seemed cautious and unsure.

One of the children in blue stepped forward and said boldly and loudly, "Take us to your leader!"

The children in red cowered before them and led them meekly to Jack the dog.

Jack proceeded to bark, lick all of the children, and romp with them for the next ten minutes.

"Who taught them that?" Dad asked Mom.

"I don't know, but they've been at it for two hours, taking different turns being the invaders and the ones who have Jack as their leader.

"I think," Dad said, "they've been watching too many Saturday morning cartoons about aliens."

Later that evening Mom brought up the afternoon play session as she talked to her husband. "I've been thinking," she said, "if aliens *did* show up in our backyard and said, "Take us to your leader," what would we do? To whom would we take them?"

"I'd definitely go with Jack," Dad said with a grin.

Do you know who is really in *control* of your life? Do you know who is in charge? Do you have just one leader? Do you have many leaders? Does your leader depend upon the environment you are in or the issue you are facing? Which leader would you turn to in an emergency or crisis?

- Why is Jesus the only true leader for the Christian?

- How do we acknowledge Him as such?

S
Supplementary Scriptures to Consider

John declared to the churches that Jesus was, is, and always will be all-powerful:

> "I am the Alpha and the Omega, the Beginning and the End,"
> says the Lord, "who is and who was and who is to come, the
> Almighty" (Rev. 1:8).

- Has there ever been a moment in your life when Jesus wasn't in charge? To what degree was He always in charge, even before you acknowledged Him as your leader? Is Jesus always in charge, even when you don't recognize that He is?

- What does the term almighty mean to you? Cite a practical manifestation of this in your life or the life of someone you know.

The Scriptures record this conversation between Moses and God about the revelation of God's glory:

> And he [Moses] said, "Please, show me Your glory."
> Then He said, "I will make all My goodness pass before you, and I will proclaim the name of the Lord before you. I will be gracious to whom I will be gracious, and I will have compassion on whom I will have compassion." But He said, "You cannot see My face; for no man shall see Me, and live." And the LORD said, "Here is a place by Me, and you shall stand on the rock. So it shall be, while My glory passes by, that I will put you in the cleft of the rock, and will cover you with My hand while I pass by. Then I will take away My hand, and you shall see My back; but My face shall not be seen"
> (Ex. 33:18–23).

• How do we attempt to make the Lord more gracious or less gracious than He is? Are there ways we attempt to make Him more or less compassionate than He is?

• What would you expect to see or experience if the Lord caused His goodness to pass before you?

• In what ways do you believe God showed His face in sending Jesus as His only begotten Son?

John recorded these words of Jesus in his Gospel account:

> [Jesus said,] "He who has seen Me has seen the Father"
> (John 14:9).

- Do you perceive that Jesus the Son and God the Father have identical character traits? If not, how do they differ?

- Do you approach Jesus the Son and God the Father in the same way as you pray? Do you hear them speaking in your mind and heart with the same voice as you read Scripture and pray?

I
Introspection and Implications

1. Which decisions, choices, and other areas of life can one have control over?

2. What does it mean to know that God is in charge of all things?

3. How do you speculate about what might happen in the future? How does the truth that Jesus is Alpha and Omega, First and Last, impact you?

C
Communicating the Good News

In what ways is it *comforting* to remember that God is in charge of all things at all times as you seek to share the gospel with an unsaved person?

In what ways is it *challenging* to remember that God is in charge of all things at all times as you seek to share the gospel with an unsaved person?

Lesson #2

COUNSEL TO THE CHURCHES IN EPHESUS AND PERGAMOS

Compromise: to accommodate differences by making concessions

B
Bible Focus

"To the angel of the church of Ephesus write,

'These things says He who holds the seven stars in His right hand, who walks in the midst of the seven golden lamp-stands: I know your works, your labor, your patience, and that you cannot bear those who are evil. And you have tested those who say they are apostles and are not, and have found them liars; and you have persevered and have patience, and have labored for My name's sake and have not become weary. Nevertheless I have this against you, that you have left your first love. Remember therefore from where you have fallen; repent and do the first works, or else I will come to you quickly and remove your lampstand from its place—unless you repent. But this you have, that you hate the deeds of the Nicolaitans, which I also hate.

He who has an ear, let him hear what the Spirit says to the churches. To him who overcomes I will give to eat from the tree of life, which is the midst of the Paradise of God."'

"And to the angel of the church in Pergamos write,

'These things says He who has the sharp two-edged sword: I know your works, and where you dwell, where Satan's throne is. And you hold fast to My name, and did not deny My faith even in the days in which Antipas was My faithful martyr, who was killed among you, where Satan dwells. But I have a few things against you, because you have there those who hold the doctrine of Balaam, who taught Balak to put a stumbling block before the children of Israel, to eat things sacrificed to idols, and to commit sexual immorality. Thus you also have those who hold the doctrine of the Nicolaitans, which thing I hate. Repent, or else I will come to you quickly and will fight against them with the sword of My mouth.

He who has an ear, let him hear what the Spirit says to the churches. To him who overcomes I will give some of the hidden manna to eat. And I will give him a white stone, and on the stone a new name written which no one knows except him who receives it" (Rev. 2:1–7, 12–17).

Ephesus was the largest and greatest city in the Roman province of Asia. Pergamos, also called Pergamum, was the official capital of the province. We have grouped these two churches in this chapter because Jesus had both praise and chastisement for each church and both churches encountered Nicolaitans.

Ephesus. The church at Ephesus was in one of the greatest cities in the world in the first century. At the time of John, Ephesus had the greatest harbor in Asia. The city was at the end of the great Spice and Silk Routes from the East, and it had a phenomenal marketplace, including the largest slave market in the region. In the first century Ephesus was known for its tremendous library, its amphitheater that seated at least ten thousand people, and for its great sports arena where the most famous games in Asia were held annually. As a free city, Ephesus was self-governed and was exempt from having Roman troops garrisoned there. Its temple devoted to the worship of Artemis, also known as Diana, was considered one of the seven wonders of the ancient world.

A number of notable Christians had ministered in Ephesus besides John, among them were Paul, Timothy, Aquila, Priscilla, and Apollos.

Jesus applauded the church at Ephesus for its hard work, its courageously steadfast endurance, and its intolerance of evil men. The downside was this: the church had lost its first love. This may have been a reference to enthusiasm for God (Jer. 2:2, 5, 11), or a reference to love having grown cold among the believers. Both can happen easily when works become the prominent focus of a body of believers or when a church finds itself embroiled in a battle against false teachers. Jesus' command was to *remember*, and to repent and return to the way things had been when the church was first established.

A tremendous thing happens when a person or a group of people intentionally *remembers* the miraculous interventions of God, interventions that involve miracles, deliverance, and above all, spiritual salvation and renewal. Nearly always there is a revival of joy, a renewed emphasis on praise, and an infusion of encouragement and edification. Jesus told the church that if it failed to return to those things it had *first loved*, it would eventually die out. We see this frequently in our world today: those churches who become works-focused and protocol-bound often exhaust themselves in their *work*. They become man-centered, not Christ-centered. We also see this when churches become so embattled against heresy that they lose sight of the great commands of God to love Him and love others, including the great commission of Christ to reach out to others with the gospel. Such churches can become places where man-generated problems become emphasized more than Christ-promised solutions, and such churches cease to be places of vibrant fellowship and ministry.

The good news for the Ephesians was that if they did remember, repent, and become overcomers, they would eat of the tree of life, a tree that symbolized the fullness of delight, wisdom, and eternity. The reward for returning to their first love was an endless marriage between God and the church that would be marked by *everlasting* love, joy, and service.

What about your church? Is it like the church at Ephesus?

What about your personal life? Have you become so weary in doing the work of ministry or contending for the faith against heresy that you have lost the peace you initially felt in coming to know the Lord or the joy you had at seeing God move in powerful ways in your life?

Pergamos. Pergamos was historically the most famous city in Asia, and at the time of John it had been the capital of the region for four hundred years. It was built on top of a cone-shaped hill, which gave the city a spectacular view in all directions. It was associated with the invention of parchment or vellum, a writing surface superior to papyrus, and through the centuries it became a religious center noted for shrines to some of the most powerful Greek gods. As a Roman administrative center, it was a city in which Caesar was widely declared to be lord, which may be what qualified it as a "seat of satan."

Jesus praised the church at Pergamos for standing strong in an environment of false worship and in the aftermath of martyrdom of one of its faithful members. But Jesus also chastised the church for *not* standing against the teachings of the Nicolaitans.

The Nicolaitans were followers of Nicolas, a proselyte of Antioch who was one of the first seven deacons in the early church (Acts 6:5). Nicolas had apparently reflected indifference about whether foods and behavioral choices were clean or unclean. The result was that his followers had extended his teaching to mean that a person could do in the flesh whatever he desired. The Nicolaitans became associated with unrestrained indulgences, immoral behavior, and eating meat offered to idols (and, in so doing, aligning themselves with pagans who saw such meals as acts of worship). Jesus likened their behavior to the false prophet Balaam who taught Balak that it was acceptable to eat meat offered to idols and to commit fornication.

Ultimately, the Nicolaitans represented compromise with the prevailing Greek culture. The Greeks were quick to engage in physical indulgences and immorality, claiming that the body and spirit were of two different origins and destinies: the body linked to earth, the spirit to heaven. The Greeks routinely engaged in ritualistic meals as part of their worship of false gods. To behave as the Greeks behaved was to say, "There is no difference in serving Christ Jesus." That message continues in many churches today, where members display no behavioral differences from the world at large but, rather, believe Christians *should* behave as the world behaves in order to identify with the world and win the world to Christ. This argument was rejected soundly by Jesus and by all of the early church fathers.

Whereas the church at Ephesus was applauded for confronting and standing against the Nicolaitans, the church at Pergamos was chastised for *not* rejecting the teachings and behavior of the Nicolaitans. Jesus said to those in Pergamos, "Repent." The consequence of not doing so meant war with the Lord. To those who did repent and overcome this heresy, Jesus promised a miraculous heavenly feast of God's wisdom (the true manna or bread that nourishes the spirit to live forever) and an eternal white stone (a symbol of being acquitted or declared innocent).

Is your church like the church at Pergamos?

What about your personal life? Are you compromising your stance for Christ by aligning yourself with worldly patterns of thinking and behaving?

The Counsel of Jesus. Note three things about the way Jesus addressed the churches.

First, Jesus had a complete message for each church, stating what He approved, what He did not approve, the action required, and both the consequence for failing to take action and the reward for doing so. Through His Word Jesus makes it no less clear what is approved, disapproved, and required of us today, as well as are the consequences and potential rewards.

Second, Jesus challenged the believers to have ears to hear what the Spirit is saying. Do not dismiss God's clear statement of what is right and wrong. Do not neglect to do what the Spirit says. We can trust God today to give us clear guidance, but we must be willing to listen to what God tells us.

Third, Jesus sent a clear message to the churches, "I know you fully." What an amazing thing to know ourselves as Jesus knows us. This is the key to confessing things we need to confess, changing things we need to change, and growing and pursuing all God has created us to be, know, have, and do. One of the greatest challenges any person ever faces is learning to see himself as Jesus sees him—both now and at his initial creation and then having the courage to pursue what Jesus sees as the fullness of one's potential.

Do you know how Jesus sees *you* today?

Do you have ears to hear what the Spirit is saying?

A
Application for Today

"Aren't you going to church this morning?" a man asked his wife, noting that she was still in her bathrobe and without makeup twenty minutes before the time they normally left for Sunday school. It wasn't like his wife to miss church. She was a faithful worker in many areas of the church, even though she also had a part-time job and was diligent in her work as a wife and the mother of their children, who were now in college.

"No," she said wearily. "I'm not going this morning."

"Are you sick?" he asked.

"Yes," she said. "I'm sick of being at church."

"You're sick of church?" he asked incredulously.

"No, not sick *of* church, sick of being *at* church. I was there on Monday to deliver some items that were needed for replenishing the church food pantry and kitchen. I was there on Tuesday for choir practice, on Wednesday for prayer meeting, on Thursday for Bible study, on Friday to arrange flowers for the altar and participate in two committee meetings scheduled back-to-back with the pastor, and on Saturday I was there to clean and prepare the things needed for the communion service. I'm too tired of doing church to do church."

"What are you going to do?" her husband asked.

"I'm going to sit in our big easy chair, turn on some soft praise music, and read my Bible. I'm going to reconnect with Jesus," she said. "I know He was there all week as I was doing these various things for the church, but I hardly said 'hello' to Him and I've been missing Him."

Do you ever get so caught up in doing what you perceive to be the *work* of the church that you lose sight of the Lord who is the head of the church?

When was the last time you felt the way you first felt after your salvation experience or spiritual rebirth? What would it take for you to reestablish overflowing joy, gratitude, and love of the Lord as your ongoing spiritual attitude?

S
Supplementary Scriptures to Consider

Repentance was not a new idea in the New Testament. A number of passages in the Old Testament call upon the faithful to receive instruction and change behavior. This passage is from the book of Proverbs:

> The ear that hears the rebukes of life
> Will abide among the wise.
> He who disdains instruction despises his own soul,
> But he who heeds rebuke gets understanding.
> The fear of the LORD is the instruction of wisdom,
> And before honor is humility (Prov. 15:31–33).

- What does it mean to "disdain instruction"? Does this include a general apathy toward learning or studying God's Word? How does disdaining instruction cause a person to despise his own soul?

- What does it mean to really hear the rebukes of life?

- How does humbling oneself to hear and obey the wisdom of the Lord lead to honor? Cite an example in your life or the life of someone you know.

Psalm 81 has been called an "Appeal for Israel's Repentance:"

> Hear, O My people, and I will admonish you.
> O Israel, if you will listen to Me.
> There shall be no foreign god among you;
> Nor shall you worship any foreign god . . . .
> But My people would not heed My voice,
> And Israel would have none of Me.
> So I gave them over to their own stubborn heart,
> To walk in their own counsels.
> Oh, that My people would listen to Me,
> That Israel would walk in My ways.
> I would soon subdue their enemies,
> And turn My hand against their adversaries.
> The haters of the LORD would pretend submission to Him,
> But their fate would endure forever.
> He would have fed them also with the finest of wheat;
> And with honey from the rock I would have satisfied you"
> (Psalm 81:8–9, 11–16).

- What happens to those who do not heed God's voice and repent of their sinful ways?

• What is the promise to those who do heed God's voice and walk in obedience to Him?

• What ultimately happens to those who have stubborn hearts and live according to their own wisdom, rather than have hearts eager to hear God's Word and live according to God's wisdom?

The prophets frequently called upon the people of God to examine their lives:

> Let us search out and examine our ways,
> And turn back to the LORD;
> Let us lift our hearts and hands
> To God in heaven (Lam. 3:40–41).

• What does it mean to examine your ways? How is it done? Why might a person be reluctant to do this?

• To repent means to "turn back to God's ways." Is there *always* an area in each person's life that is in need of being turned back toward the Lord? Are we ever fully beyond the need to search out and examine our ways and repent?

• To lift one's heart is to have an attitude of worship and adoration; to lift one's hands to do deeds that give praise to God. How might a Christian today *daily* lift both heart and hands to the Lord?

I
Introspection and Implications

1. Do you see yourself as Jesus sees you? As you are today? As you might be one day? How did you come to see yourself as Jesus sees you? What did that insight cause you to change in your life? If you do not see yourself as Jesus sees you, how might you gain His perspective on your life?

2. Is there a tendency to hear the negative evaluation of another person—or of Christ Jesus—more strongly than we hear a positive evaluation? What does it mean to you that Jesus noted the positive aspects of the churches before calling their attention to the things that needed to be changed? What do you believe are your strengths, spiritually, mentally, emotionally, relationally, experientially, physically?

3. Do you know what Jesus is calling you to change in your thinking, believing, or behavior? If so, how will you pursue those changes? If not, how might you gain this knowledge?

4. What do you do to refresh yourself spiritually when you feel weary in your walk of faith?

5. Respond to this statement: "The danger in being identical to the world is that the world fails to see any difference Christ Jesus makes in a person's life."

6. Have you ever been so tired of fighting for what's right or speaking out against heresy that you feel like giving up? What did you do? What was the outcome—for you, for others of like faith, for those who were in error?

7. Have you ever felt like you were compromising with the world in your thinking or decision-making? In your attitudes? In your behavior? How did you feel? What did you do?

8. How do you know that you are really hearing what the *Spirit* is saying to you?

C
Communicating the Good News

How can we use postmodern ways of communicating the gospel without compromising its message?

Are there any church heresies or compromises that have crept into your congregation that need to be addressed?

"Jesus sees who you have been, who you are and, most importantly, who you might be in Him." Respond to this line of argument as an approach to evangelistic ministry. How might this statement be the foundation for a discipleship program?

LESSON #3

COUNSEL TO THE CHURCHES IN THYATIRA, SARDIS, AND LAODICEA

Jezebel: wicked idolatrous queen in Old Testament times; generally used to refer to a person or a group of people who advocate unrestrained immorality, idolatry, and worship of false gods

B
Bible Focus

"And to the angel of the church in Thyatira write,

'These things says the Son of God, who has eyes like a flame of fire, and His feet like fine brass: I know your works, love, service, faith, and your patience; and as for your works, the last are more than the first. Nevertheless I have a few things against you, because you allow that woman Jezebel, who calls herself a prophetess, to teach and seduce My servants to commit sexual immorality and eat things sacrificed to idols. And I gave her time to repent of her sexual immorality, and she did not repent. Indeed I will cast her into a sickbed, and those who commit adultery with her into great tribulation, unless they repent of their deeds. I will kill her children with death, and all the churches shall know that I am He who searches the minds and hearts. And I will give to each one of you according to your works.

Now to you I say, and to the rest of Thyatira, as many as do not have this doctrine, who have not known the depths of Satan, as they say, I will put on you no other burden. But hold fast what you have till I come. And he who overcomes, and keeps My works until the end, to him I will give power over the nations—

'He shall rule them with a rod of iron;

They shall be dashed to pieces like the potter's vessels'—

as I also have received from My Father, and I will give him the morning star.

He who has an ear, let him hear what the Spirit says to the churches."'

"And to the angel of the church in Sardis write,

'These things says He who has the seven Spirits of God and the seven stars: "I know your works, that you have a name that you are alive, but you are dead. Be watchful, and strengthen the things which remain, that are ready to die, for I have not found your works perfect before God. Remember therefore how you have received and heard; hold fast and repent. Therefore if you will not watch, I will come upon you as a thief, and you will not know what hour I will come upon you. You have a few names even in Sardis who have not defiled their garments; and they shall walk with Me in white, for they are worthy. He who overcomes shall be clothed in white garments, and I will not blot out his name from the Book of

Life; but I will confess his name before My Father and before His angels.

He who has an ear, let him hear what the Spirit says to the churches."'

"And to the angel of the church of the Laodiceans write,

'These things says the Amen, the Faithful and True Witness, the Beginning of the creation of God: I know your works, that you are neither cold nor hot. I could wish you were cold or hot. So then, because you are lukewarm, and neither cold nor hot, I will vomit you out of My mouth. Because you say, 'I am rich, have become wealthy, and have need of nothing'—and do not know that you are wretched, miserable, poor, blind, and naked—I counsel you to buy from Me gold refined in the fire, that you may be rich; and white garments, that you may be clothed, that the shame of your nakedness may not be re-vealed; and anoint your eyes with eye salve, that you may see. As many as I love, I rebuke and chasten. Therefore be zealous and repent. Behold, I stand at the door and knock. If anyone hears My voice and opens the door, I will come in to him and dine with him, and he with Me. To him who overcomes I will grant to sit with Me on My throne, as I also overcame and sat down with My Father on His throne.

He who has an ear, let him hear what the Spirit says to the churches"'" (Rev. 2:18—3:6, 14–22).

These three churches are grouped together in our study because of Jesus' strong chastisement and words of judgment. Jesus had very specific issues with these believers. They were in grave danger.

Thyratira. Thyratira was located along a major trade route, and it pro-vided a first line of defense for the capital Pergamos. The city had no special religious or political significance. It was, however, known for commerce and a large number of trade guilds—among them were guilds for workers in wool, linen, bronze, and leather; dyers, potters, bakers, seamstresses, and slave-dealers.

Jesus commended the believers there for their love, loyalty, service, and endurance. He noted they were growing in their works for the kingdom. Then He chastised them for failing to deal with Jezebel. The name of the woman at the heart of the error was likely not Jezebel. This was a term used for any person who promoted the worship of false gods, as Queen Jezebel had done in the time of King Ahab. It is most likely that this woman was pleading for compromise with the world's standards when it came to busi-ness and commercial prosperity. The problem involved the requirements of membership for a commercial guild: participation in common meals, often held in the temple of a false god and often involving meat offered to idols. The meals were perceived to be acts of worship to the false god that supposedly aided the guild, and often ended in drunken revelry and immoral acts. The sin of Jezebel in Thyratira was that, under the guise of being a prophetess, she tried to get the church members to participate in these practices. She claimed that it was God's will for the believers to engage in this form of compromise with the world's commercial system.

Jesus strongly denounced Jezebel and those who heeded her, and He stated that the consequence for not turning away from her would be death. To those who had not participated in the sin she advocated and who were overcomers of her influence, the Lord promised that they would exert authority over the Gentiles and be given "the morning star," a bright witness of righteousness after the darkest hours of a spiritual night.

Is your church like the church at Thyratira?

What about your personal life? Are you following someone who is encouraging you to compromise with the ways of the world to your spiritual detriment? If people looked at your life would they see any difference from your non-believing neighbors or co-workers?

Sardis. Seven hundred years before Christ, Sardis was one of the greatest cities of the world. It had legendary wealth, which had survived devastating earthquakes and major invasions by Persia, Alexander the Great, and Rome. At the time of John's letter, the city was wealthy but degenerate. The Sardians were noted for being lazy and lackluster and generally lethargic about things that mattered most. This general malaise had infected the church.

Jesus' only praise for the church at Sardis was that a few people had not defiled themselves. The chastisement of Jesus fell on this church because it had a reputation for life but was actually spiritually dead. They were an incomplete work. Jesus called them to awaken and diligently seek to grow in their faith and in their works for the kingdom of God. If they didn't, Christ himself would come and take away what had been given them: His presence and His Word. Perhaps the saddest aspect of this would be that the Sardians would be so soundly asleep that they wouldn't even know Christ had come and stripped them of the genuine spiritual power or wisdom they once had.

Those who were faithful were given a threefold promise. First, they would be clothed in white robes, which were generally associated with victory, purity, and celebration. Such robes were traditionally given to those who were baptized to signify their new life in Christ. Jesus also promised that their names would remain in the Book of Life—they would be registered among the faithful citizens in the kingdom of God—and Jesus would confess their names before the Father. All of these are references to a spiritual revival, a renewal of spiritual life that produces conversions, new commitments to grow in Christ and live in purity, and a surge of courage to spread the gospel in new ways.

Is your church like the church at Sardis? Has your church become spiritually lethargic—perhaps trusting in wealth or prosperity to signify that the church is acceptable before the Lord?

What about your personal life? What are the indicators that you are spiritually alive?

Laodicea. The importance of Laodicea was directly related to its location on the major trade route from Ephesus to the east. It had become a great commercial center known especially for clothing manufacturing, a financial and banking center, and a medical center. It had a very large Jewish population.

Of the seven churches to whom Jesus spoke, the church at Laodicea is the only one about whom He said nothing positive. Jesus chastised the church for failing to take a stand on matters of eternal importance. The church may have adopted a stance of neutrality on any issue considered controversial in the city. Or it may have become totally indifferent and apathetic toward human need. Either way, the church had become tepid and was nauseating to the Lord.

Jesus also chastised the church members for relying so heavily upon their own wealth, to the point that they felt no need for the Lord's power to work in and through them. Jesus admonished them to seek and acquire

- refined gold—true spiritual riches

- white garments—reflecting spiritual purity

- eye salve—to take away blindness or dimness of sight and thus, have a renewed ability to see and pursue what is right and wrong and what is needed by others

These were direct references to the financial, clothing, and medical industries for which the city had gained great reputation. Jesus was clearly calling the church to trust Him for spiritual wealth and power, forgiveness on the basis of God's mercy and not human works, and healing that leads to genuine wholeness.

Those who failed to do so would be "vomited" out of the Lord's mouth and be subjected to great rebuke and chastisement. Those who repented and opened the door to the Lord's presence would enjoy great fellowship with Christ and sit with Him in judgment. Jesus said that He was standing at the door, knocking. He was not utterly rejecting the Laodiceans. Rather, He desired greater spiritual intimacy with them.

Is your church like the church at Laodicea?

What about your personal life? Do you trust in your own abilities and accomplishments more than in the Lord? Have you become lukewarm in your walk with Christ Jesus and your commitment to Him?

A
Application for Today

"Now what?" Dad asked as he came home and saw his children quietly at play.

"Shhhhh," Mom cautioned, putting her finger to her lips.

"What's with all the quiet?" Dad whispered. The children were moving slowly and deliberately, with exaggerated motions. They were making very little noise. It certainly wasn't the highly verbal and energetic play scene Dad was accustomed to seeing in the family's back yard.

After a few minutes he called to his children, "Are you kids having fun?"

The oldest child looked at Dad with both surprise and a touch of disapproval. "No, Dad," he said rather sternly. "We aren't supposed to be having *fun*. We're playing church."

How easy is it for a church to lose its spiritual zeal and for many or most of its members not to recognize that the loss is occurring or has occurred?

How do you define an "alive" church? Cite several hallmarks that describe such a church. How does your church rate against the criteria you have identified?

What are the hallmarks of a spiritually "alive" person? Are they the same hallmarks as those for a church body? How do *you* rate against this criteria?

S
Supplementary Scriptures to Consider

The writer of the book of Proverbs had this to say about chastening:

> "My son, do not despise the chastening of the LORD,
> Nor detest His correction;
> For whom the LORD loves He corrects,
> Just as a father the son in whom he delights (Prov. 3:11–12).

- How do you define *chasten* in everyday terms? (Note: one dictionary definition is "to subject to discipline, often subduing a self-centered or self-directed attitude.")

- Can a person encourage himself when he is feeling chastened? In what ways might a person encourage himself? In what ways might other believers offer effective encouragement?

- Why is correction a necessary expression of genuine parental or godly love?

To what ends should correction always be aimed?

- What is the most effective way to correct a beloved child?

The writer of Hebrews saw chastening as a sign that a person was a genuine child of God:

> If you endure chastening, God deals with you as with sons; for what son is there whom a father does not chasten? But if you are without chastening, of which all have become partakers, then you are illegitimate and not sons (Heb. 12:7–8).

• Is a person who never feels chastened by God in any way a genuine believer in Christ Jesus? Why?

• Has the Holy Spirit convicted or counseled you in a way that might be considered chastening?

The apostle Paul gave a very clear portrait of those who are subject to judgment and the purposes of God in chastening those He loves:

> We know that the judgment of God is according to truth against those who practice such things. And do you think this, O man, you who judge those practicing such things, and doing the same, that you will escape the judgment of God? Or do you despise the riches of His goodness, forbearance, and longsuffering, not knowing that the goodness of God leads you to repentance? But in accordance with your hardness and your impenitent heart you are treasuring up for yourself wrath in the day of wrath and revelation of the righteous judgment of God, who "will render to each one according to his deeds": eternal life to those who by patient continuance in doing good seek for glory, honor, and immortality; but to those who are self-seeking and do not obey the truth, but obey unrighteous-ness—indignation and wrath, tribulation and anguish, on every soul of man who does evil, of the Jew first and also of the Greek; but glory, honor, and peace to everyone who works what is good, to the Jew first and also to the Greek. For there is no partiality with God" (Rom. 2:2–11).

• When Paul wrote about "practicing such things" he was referring to a list he had just given the Romans of examples of the behavior exhibited by those with debased minds: "unrighteousness, sexual immorality, wickedness, covetousness, maliciousness; full of envy, murder, strife, deceit, evil-mindedness; they are whisperers, backbiters, haters of God, violent, proud boasters, inventors of evil things, disobedient to parents, undiscerning, untrustworthy, unloving, unforgiving, unmerciful." (Rom. 1:29–31.) Read through this list carefully. Are you subject to judgment for participating in any of these?

• God desires that His children *repent* of those things that produce judgment. The impenitent person shows no regret or sorrow for sin or misbehavior. Have you ever encountered a person who showed no sorrow for their sin? What is the danger such a person faces?

• Some people seem to believe they are entitled to special favor from God. What would the apostle Paul say to such a person?

The apostle Paul also wrote this to the Corinthian church:

For godly sorrow produces repentance leading to salvation, not to be regretted; but the sorrow of the world produces death (2 Cor. 7:10).

• In everyday terms, how do you define "godly sorrow"?

• Why will a Christian never regret repentance?

• How does the sorrow of the world differ from godly sorrow? In what ways does the sorrow of the world produce death? (*Note*: consider the person who says "I'm sorry" and means "I'm sorry I got caught," rather than "I'm sorry for what I did.")

I
Introspection and Implications

1. Jesus said to the Laodiceans, "I could wish you were cold or hot" (Rev. 3:15). Some Bible scholars interpret this as a reference to the heat associated with convicting and healing power, and the refreshing coolness associated with spiritual rejuvenation. In any case, the Laodiceans were not willing to take a stand in any particular direction – they were completely compromised and ineffective as a church. Given this general metaphor, what temperature do you believe you are? Is your faith hot enough to bring a sense of conviction or healing to others? Do others who are weary in their faith walk turn to you for spiritual refreshment?

2. Jesus said to the Laodiceans, "If anyone hears My voice and opens the door, I will come in to him and dine with him, and he with Me" (Rev. 3:20). To share a meal with a person in ancient times was a sign of trust, loyalty, affection, and intimacy. In what ways do you dine with the Lord? How do you experience affection and intimacy with Him? Do you have a sense that the Lord trusts you and is loyal to you, even as you trust Him and are loyal to Him?

3. What do you do if you sense that there are things that need to be corrected in your church in order for your church to be fully pleasing to the Lord—but nobody in a leadership position seems to sense what you are sensing?

4. There is no indication in the book of Revelation that there was more than one body of believers in each of these cities addressed by Jesus. That meant a believer had no recourse in choosing with whom he might want to associate for worship. What does a righteous person do, in a righteous way, to bring about repentance and renewal of faith in a church that has fallen into serious error?

5. What challenges do you face when you work or conduct your personal business in an environment that is not godly? Have you ever experienced a temptation to compromise with the world's systems? What happened?

C
Communicating the Good News

Given the fact that there are no perfect churches—primarily because there are no perfect people and it takes perfect people to create and maintain a perfect church—what do you say to the unsaved person who doesn't like Christians?

LESSON #4

AFFIRMATION TO THE CHURCHES IN SMYRNA AND PHILADELPHIA

Overcome: persevere through challenges to gain the victory; to struggle successfully against an adversary and win

B
Bible Focus

> *"And to the angel of the church in Smyrna write,*
> *'These things says the First and the Last, who was dead,*
> *and came to life: I know your works, tribulation, and poverty*
> *(but you are rich); and I know the blasphemy of those who say*
> *they are Jews and are not, but are a synagogue of Satan. Do*
> *not fear any of those things which you are about to suffer.*
> *Indeed, the devil is about to throw some of you into prison,*
> *that you may be tested, and you will have tribulation ten days.*
> *Be faithful until death, and I will give you the crown of life.*
>
> *He who has an ear, let him hear what the Spirit says to the*
> *churches. He who overcomes shall not be hurt by the second*
> *death.*
> *And to the angel of the church in Philadelphia write,*
> *'These things says He who is holy, He who is true, "He who*
> *has the key of David, He who opens and no one shuts, and*
> *shuts and no one opens": I know your works. See, I have set*
> *before you an open door, and no one can shut it; for you have*
> *a little strength, have kept My word, and have not denied My*
> *name. Indeed I will make those of the synagogue of Satan,*
> *who say they are Jews and are not, but lie—indeed I will make*
> *them come and worship before your feet, and to know that I*
> *have loved you. Because you have kept My command to*
> *persevere, I also will keep you from the hour of trial which*
> *shall come upon the whole world, to test those who dwell on*
> *the earth. Behold, I am coming quickly. Hold fast what you*
> *have, that no one may take your crown. He who overcomes, I*
> *will make him a pillar in the temple of My God, and he shall*
> *go out no more. I will write on him the name of My God and*
> *the name of the city of My God, the New Jerusalem, which*
> *comes down out of heaven from My God. And I will write on*
> *him My new name.*
>
> *He who has an ear, let him hear what the Spirit says to the*
> *churches"' (Rev. 2:8–11; 3:7–13).*

These last two churches addressed by Jesus are grouped together because
Jesus had no complaints against these churches. What an awesome and
wonderful thing to be in a church that has the full approval of the Lord.

Smyrna. Smyrna was considered the most beautiful city in Asia Minor. It
had the most secure and convenient harbor, a nearly constant western breeze,
and a setting on foothills dotted with majestic buildings. It was, perhaps, one

of the earliest planned cities in history, with wide, paved streets, artistic fountains, and majestic architecture for its temples and public buildings. It was noted for trade, religious eminence, and culture.

This is not to say everything was lovely for the church in Smyrna. The large Jewish populace there was especially hostile to the church. As a result, many of the Christians were shut out of commercial trade agreements and their businesses suffered as a result. The phrase "synagogue of satan" means "assembly of satan. This was a twist of the expression the Jews used for themselves as an "assembly of the Lord." Jesus stood strongly against their persecution of the church and identified them as the enemy. Jesus foretold the believers they would be persecuted even further; some of them would even go to prison for a short period. However, Jesus promised that, if they remained loyal and endured even to death, He would give them the unfading crown of eternal life.

Jesus encouraged the believers to have no *fear* of what they might experience but to remain steadfast in their trust of Him.

Is your church like the church at Smyrna? Are there people in your church who are being shut out of the prevailing prosperity of your city because of their faith?

What about your personal life? Are you facing the possibility of increased persecution for Christ? Are you preparing yourself to persevere in faith through whatever may happen?

Philadelphia. Philadelphia was the youngest of the seven cities Jesus addressed. It was founded to take the Greek culture and language to the cities of Lydia and Phrygia. Through the years it had succeeded in doing so. The city was established in an area of extinct volcanoes, which made for excellent vineyards and wine production. In the first century, it experienced a number of earthquakes, some of them highly destructive.

Jesus said that He was setting before the Philadelphian Christians an open door that no person could shut, a divine opportunity for tremendous witness. Some of this opportunity for witness was probably related to the Christians' firm faith and trust in the Lord during times of natural disaster. Jesus foretold that even the Jews who had persecuted the Christians would fall before them seeking to know more about what gave them such enduring faith.

Jesus promised this church that if it continued to endure, the Lord would give the believers settled serenity and make them a pillar of strength that all would recognize.

Is your church like the church at Philadelphia? Is your church a beacon of solid and lasting faith in troubled times?

What about your personal life? Are you looking for all of the open doors the Lord may be setting before you as opportunities to share the gospel?

A
Application for Today

Much of the small town on the banks of the river was under water. The home of a young woman named Sue was no exception. She had at least two feet of water on the ground floor of her house. Fortunately, she had been able to move her prized possessions to the upper floor of her home, load up her car, hitch her small fishing boat and its trailer to her vehicle, and drive to higher ground before the river topped its banks.

Once on higher ground, Sue launched her little boat into the rising waters and went from house to house, seeking any residents of her community who may have thought they could ride out the flood in the upper floors of their homes. She helped rescue at least eight people and several of their pets before emergency crews arrived on the scene. Her final rescue was an elderly man who was connected to a breathing machine. She helped him get to a hospital in a nearby community that was not in danger of flooding.

Fully assured that nobody else in her flooded neighborhood needed her help, Sue went to the emergency shelter and began to work alongside Red Cross and other volunteers to help as much as possible. She worked long hours helping to prepare meals, pass out bed linens, and play with young children so their parents could get a few hours sleep.

What was so remarkable is that Sue is a paraplegic. She cannot use her legs. She is confined to a wheelchair, and has a small chair lift on the staircase in her home.

After the crisis had passed and people began to return to their homes, a number of people came to thank Sue. A reporter asked her how she had found the strength to help so many people in so many ways. She said, "When I had the accident that took away my legs, countless people helped me, some of whom I didn't even know and still don't know. This was my turn to help. Jesus Christ gave me the strength. In fact, I felt more strength than I have felt in years. I know it was the Lord."

The story about Sue made the nightly news and a community newspaper. Eighteen people sought out Sue to know more about Jesus during the next few months. Twelve of them accepted Jesus and joined the church Sue attended. The remaining six renewed their commitment to serving the Lord and became more active in their churches.

A Christian's light often shines the brightest in times of great crisis. It seems there is rarely a shortage of difficulty in our world.

How might you volunteer in a difficult situation to help others and, in the process, find open doors for giving witness to Christ Jesus?

S
Supplementary Scriptures to Consider

The writer of the book of Hebrews regarded God as a reward-giver:

> Without faith it is impossible to please Him, for he who comes
> to God must believe that He is, and that He is a rewarder of
> those who diligently seek him (Heb. 11:6).

• In what ways is it important that we see God as being a rewarder and not
solely a judge or punisher?

• What is the balance between God's justice and God's mercy? Between
God's judgments and God's rewards?

In addressing the church at Philadelphia, Jesus referenced these words
from the prophet Isaiah:

> The key of the house of David I will lay on his shoulder;
> So he shall open, and no one shall shut;
> And he shall shut, and no one shall open (Is. 22:22).

• This statement in Isaiah was made to Eliakim, the appointed chief steward
of King David. It signified that he would be authorized to exercise full
authority in administering the affairs of David's palace, having access to
every area of the palace and all of the wealth in it. Jesus has access to all
that belongs to God the Father, including all the riches of both heaven and
earth. What does it mean TO be in relationship with the One who has
access to everything that is good and necessary for both early life and
eternal life?

- The church of Philadelphia was given an open door by Jesus who is the One capable of opening *all* the doors to God's goodness. What do you believe was being given to this church?

- The door that was opened to the Philadelphians was, in some way, a door of opportunity and transition. What opportunities do you believe still lie ahead for you as a Christian? For your church? What transitions do you personally anticipate in the years ahead? For your church?

Elsewhere in the book of Revelation, we find these words related to being an overcomer:

> Then I heard a loud voice saying in heaven, "Now salvation, and strength, and the kingdom of our God, and the power of His Christ have come, for the accuser of our brethren, who accused them before our God day and night, has been cast down. And they overcame him by the blood of the Lamb and by the word of their testimony, and they did not love their lives to the death" (Rev. 12:10–11).

- Describe in your own terms what it means to you to overcome the enemy of your soul:

By the blood of the Lamb:

By the word of your testimony:

By not loving your life to the death:

Toward the end of the book of Revelation, we find this promise to those who overcome evil:

> And He said to me, "It is done. I am the Alpha and the Omega the Beginning and the End. I will give of the fountain of the water of life freely to him who thirsts. He who overcomes shall inherit all things, and I will be his God and he shall be My son. But the cowardly, unbelieving, abominable, murderers, sexually immoral, sorcerers, idolaters, and all liars shall have their part in the lake which burns with fire and brimstone, which is the second death" (Rev. 21:6–8).

• What is it the believer overcomes? Are human lusts and propensities toward evil part of what a Christian overcomes?

Given the list of descriptors for those who enter the second death, how might a Christian overcome:

Lack of courage:

Lack of belief:

Things God calls abominable:

Things that kill (others and self):

Sexual immorality:

Sorcery (practices associated with the occult):

Idolatry (trusting other things more than or equal to God):

Lying:

I
Introspection and Implications

1. Jesus said to the church of Philadelphia that those who were overcomers would have three names written on them: the name of God (identifying them as God's own people), the name of the city of God (identifying them of citizens of God's everlasting kingdom, with access to His everlasting presence), and the new name of Jesus. Revelation 19:12 tells us that we will not know this new name of Jesus until Christ conquers all, but this new name will give the person full access to all that Christ wins in His triumph over evil. The people of Philadelphia knew a great deal about taking on a new name. The city had once been called Neocaesarea (New City of Caesar) and later Flavia (in honor of Vespasian). Have you ever experienced a change of name? What was your experience with name change? How might being given a new name change the way a person defines or values himself? What names are written on your life?

2. Jesus honored the Philadelphians because they "kept My word, and have not denied My name" (Rev. 3:8). What does it mean to keep God's word? What does it mean, in your everyday life, to not deny the name of the Lord?

3. Do you consider yourself to be an overcomer? In what ways? On the basis of what criteria? Do you believe Jesus sees you as an overcomer? What are the rewards you can expect from Jesus for being an overcomer *from His perspective?*

C
Communicating the Good News

What part of Jesus' message to the churches at Smyrna and Philadelphia might be good to include in an evangelistic message aimed at those who don't know Christ?

LESSON #5

PRAISE IN THE THRONE ROOM OF HEAVEN

Praise: verbally giving honor to God for
His unchanging attributes and works

B
Bible Focus

> *After these things I looked, and behold, a door standing*
> *open in heaven. And the first voice which I heard was like a*
> *trumpet speaking with me, saying, "Come up here, and I will*
> *show you things which must take place after this."*
>
> *Immediately I was in the Spirit; and behold, a throne set in*
> *heaven, and One sat on the throne. And He who sat there was*
> *like a jasper and sardius stone in appearance; and there was a*
> *rainbow around the throne, in appearance like an emerald.*
> *Around the throne were twenty-four thrones, and on the*
> *thrones I saw twenty-four elders sitting, clothed in white*
> *robes, and they had crowns of gold on their heads. And from*
> *the throne proceeded lightnings, thunderings, and voices.*
> *Seven lamps of fire were burning before the throne, which are*
> *the seven Spirits of God.*
>
> *Before the throne there was a sea of glass, like crystal. And*
> *in the midst of the throne, and around the throne, were four*
> *living creatures full of eyes in front and in back. The first*
> *living creature was like a lion, the second living creature like*
> *a calf, the third living creature had a face like a man, and the*
> *fourth living creature was like a flying eagle. The four living*
> *creatures, each having six wings, were full of eyes around and*
> *within. And they do not rest day or night, saying:*
>
> > *"Holy, holy, holy,*
> > *Lord God Almighty,*
> > *Who was and is and is to come."*
>
> *Whenever the living creatures give glory and honor and*
> *thanks to Him who sits on the throne, who lives forever and*
> *ever, the twenty-four elders fall down before Him who sits on*
> *the throne and worship Him who lives forever and ever, and*
> *cast their crowns before the throne, saying:*
>
> > *"You are worthy, O Lord,*
> > *To receive glory and honor and power;*
> > *For You created all things,*
> > *And by Your will they exist and were created"*
> > *(Rev. 4:1–11).*

Of one thing we can be certain: Heaven is filled with praise.

We may not be able to fully comprehend the visual glories of the throne
room of God—there may be colors there that are not part of our earthly
spectrum of light, and there may be objects and creatures there that are not

part of God's creation on planet Earth—but we can know this from the book of Revelation:

First, everybody and every thing honors and worships God. The implication is that we will all have opportunity to praise God in His throne room. The twenty-four elders is likely a reference to the fact that the priests who served in the temple in Jerusalem were divided into twenty-four different teams. Each team had its own leader, and each team served for a set period in offering sacrifices. The sacrifice of praise will involve all believers.

Second, heaven is filled with praise. The sound of heaven is the sound of verbal praise. The praise is a three-fold doxology:

- We will praise God for His *holiness.* God is different from man in ways that are mysterious and unfathomable, higher and greater. The supreme holiness of the Trinity is expressed: holy, holy, holy.

- We will praise God for His *omnipotence.* He is Almighty. He has the ability to create all that He desires to create and the ability to control and govern all that He creates. Nothing can withstand His power or thwart His purposes.

- We will praise God for His *eternal and everlasting nature.* His existence is constant and above any fluctuation of time and season. God has always been, is now, and will be forever.

John saw in his vision that those who fell before God in worship also cast their crowns before His throne. A crown refers to anything that is an expression of human achievements such as fame, recognition, honors, or a position of power. Those who worship God recognize that He is the One who gave them any ability they have to achieve anything beneficial. He is the One who allowed them to have notoriety so they might uplift His Name. He is the One who allowed them to rise to a position of power so they might enact good. We one day will yield all of our best and highest honors to the Lord, in full recognition that He holds first place in the entire universe. He is the One who created us for and enabled us to fulfill His purposes.

What is your response to God's holiness?

What is your response to God's power?

What is your response to God's everlastingness?

What is your response to the truth that all that you are and all that you have accomplished is ultimately the work of God?

A
Application for Today

"Whatcha doin'?" a boy asked his older sister. She had been singing in front of her bedroom mirror, apparently a new song of her own creation, both lyrics and melody.

"Rehearsing," the girl replied.

"Rehearsing for what?" her brother asked.

"For the big concert," the girl replied.

"But that isn't a song," the boy protested. "You're just making up words and giving them a tune."

"So?" the girl said.

"So, who's going to want you to sing that in a concert?" the boy asked.

"Did you hear what I've been singing?" the girl asked in reply.

"Yeah," the boy said. "It sounded like stuff about Jesus."

"Right." The girl said. "My Sunday school teacher told us last week that we are going to be singing praise songs when we come into God's throne room. She said that praise is one thing we do here on the earth that we will continue to do in heaven. I'm getting ready."

The boy sat in silence, trying to think of a response. The girl quickly added, "You might want to do some rehearsing of your own."

For what are you voicing praise today?

Have you ever created a praise song? Give it a try.

S
Supplementary Scriptures to Consider

The book of Revelation erupts into a number of praise songs, including this one:

> And I saw in the right hand of Him who sat on the throne a
> scroll written inside and on the back, sealed with seven seals
> . . . . Now when He had taken the scroll, the four living
> creatures and the twenty-four elders fell down before the
> Lamb, each having a harp, and golden bowls full of incense,
> which are the prayers of the saints. And they sang a new song,
> saying:
>
> > "You are worthy to take the scroll,
> > And to open its seals;
> > For You were slain,
> > And have redeemed us to God by Your blood

Out of every tribe and tongue and people and nation,
And have made us kings and priests to our God;
And we shall reign on the earth" (Rev. 5:1, 8–10).

• What do you praise Jesus for doing on your behalf? In your life? Through you for others?

All of the living beings in heaven were heard singing this song to Jesus:

Then I looked, and I heard the voice of many angels around the throne, the living creatures, and the elders; and the number of them was ten thousand times ten thousand, and thousands of thousands, saying with a loud voice:

"Worthy is the Lamb who was slain
To receive power and riches and wisdom,
And strength and honor and glory and blessing"
(Rev. 5:11–12).

• Reflect on how you consider Jesus to be the source of these things:

Power:

Riches:

Wisdom:

Strength:

Honor:

Glory:

Blessing:

John heard every creature on heaven, on earth, and under the earth voicing praise:

> And every creature which is in heaven and on the earth and under the earth and such as are in the sea, and all that are in them, I heard saying:
>
> > "Blessing and honor and glory and power
> > Be to Him who sits on the throne,
> > And to the Lamb, forever and ever"
> > (Rev. 5:13).

• Write an expression of praise from your own heart:

The word *Amen* literally means *so be it* or *may it be so:*

> Then the four living creatures said, "Amen." And the twenty-four elders fell down and worshiped Him who lives forever and ever (Rev. 5:14).

• In what ways will the *Amen* we voice in heaven be our final *Amen*?

John heard special praise being voiced to God for salvation:

> After these things I looked, and behold, a great multitude which no one could number, of all nations, tribes, peoples, and tongues, standing before the throne and before the Lamb, clothed with white robes, with palm branches in their hands, and crying out with a loud voice, saying, "Salvation belongs to our God who sits on the throne, and to the Lamb." All the angels stood around the throne and the elders and the four living creatures, and fell on their faces before the throne and worshiped God, saying:
>
> > "Amen. Blessing and glory and wisdom,
> > Thanksgiving and honor and power and might,
> > Be to our God forever and ever.
> > Amen." (Rev. 7:9–12)

• For what specific things related to your *salvation* do you give thanks and praise? (In other words, what do you believe the Lord saved you from?)

Specific praise was also given for God's judgment and rewards:

> Then the seventh angel sounded: And there were loud voices in heaven, saying, "The kingdoms of this world have become the kingdoms of our Lord and of His Christ, and He shall reign forever and ever." And the twenty-four elders who sat

before God on their thrones fell on their faces and worshiped God, saying:

"We give You thanks, O Lord God Almighty,
The One who is and who was and who is to come,
Because You have taken Your great power and reigned.
The nations were angry, and Your wrath has come,
And the time of the dead, that they should be judged,
 And that You should reward Your servants the prophets and
   the saints,
And those who fear Your name, small and great,
And should destroy those who destroy the earth"
(Rev. 11:15–18).

- What do you believe will cease once Jesus comes to rule and reign over all nations? Make a list of at least ten items. Then, offer your thanks to God for the judgment He will make.

I
Introspection and Implications

1. Is offering praise and thanksgiving part of your daily prayer life? If not, how might you establish greater praise and thanksgiving as a spiritual discipline? If so, what does a daily offering of praise and thanksgiving mean to you?

2. In what ways do *you* benefit from offering praise and thanksgiving to God?

3. "The voicing of praise and thanksgiving is an act of God's own creative power displayed by one of His created beings." How do you respond to this statement?

C
Communicating the Good News

Why is it important that we have an attitude of thanksgiving and praise as we tell others about Jesus Christ?

LESSON #6

VICTORY OVER SATAN
AND ALL GOD'S ENEMIES

*Satan: originally a Babylonian word for adversary;
a snitch, a betrayer, an accuser; name for the
enemy who opposes God's people
Devil: liar, deceiver, tempter*

B
Bible Focus

> *And war broke out in heaven: Michael and his angels*
> *fought with the dragon; and the dragon and his angels fought,*
> *but they did not prevail, nor was a place found for them in*
> *heaven any longer. So the great dragon was cast out, that*
> *serpent of old, called the Devil and Satan, who deceives the*
> *whole world; he was cast to the earth, and his angels were*
> *cast out with him.*
>
> *Then I heard a loud voice saying in heaven, "Now salva-*
> *tion, and strength, and the kingdom of our God, and the power*
> *of His Christ have come, for the accuser of our brethren, who*
> *accused them before our God day and night, has been cast*
> *down. And they overcame him by the blood of the Lamb and*
> *by the word of their testimony, and they did not love their lives*
> *to the death (Rev. 12:7–11).*

One thing we can conclude with certainty from the book of Revelation is that the enemy of our souls is one day going to be destroyed definitively, absolutely, completely, and forever. He will have no more influence on us, any other person, any human system, or any aspect of creation. All of the evil he embodies will end. With his demise is the final demise of all that destroys or damages God's creation and all that tempts mankind.

The above passage from Revelation uses five terms for our spiritual enemy:

- *Satan.* This term is generally presented throughout the Scriptures as the proper name given to the archangel Lucifer once he had rebelled against God and was cast from heaven. In the Old Testament, satan is depicted as an angel who remains under God's command even after his fall, and he retains access to God's throne room. The term satan literally means *adversary*: one who not only voices prosecution against someone but who brings about the need for prosecution and devises all things that lead to a person's condemnation before God. When Israel fell to Babylonian conquest, men called "satans" infiltrated the Jewish community that remained in Jerusalem, seeking to determine who might be planning an uprising against Babylon. The word took on the meaning of "snitch." The great tactic of satan is the exertion of constant pressure to be perfect (wise, strong, and whole) apart from God's help.

- *Devil.* This is generally a New Testament word from the Greek word *diabolos*, which means slanderer or liar. The devil is the tempter and the seducer, the one who uses every wile to lead humanity astray and hinder the work of the saints in spreading the gospel. The great tactic of the devil is deceit.

• *Great Dragon.* The term *dragon* focuses on the fact that our enemy is a creature made by God. He certainly is never on equal footing with God in any area of power or influence. Dragons that breathed fire are not entirely mythological; such reptiles in various sizes apparently existed in ancient times. Small dragon-like creatures have been found in remote areas of the world in the past century. Dragons were considered the fiercest enemy man faced in the animal kingdom because they could not be readily controlled, captured, or placated. Ancient dragon lore depicted these animals as having wings and being brilliant in color. Part of the devil's curse in the Garden of Eden was, "on your belly you shall go, and you shall eat dust" (Gen. 3:14). Some Bible scholars believe the devil was a dragon that was stripped of wings and feet and became serpent at the time of the Fall. The great tactic of the dragon is fear.

• *Serpent of Old.* This serpent is the one in the Garden of Eden that God allowed to retain power to "bruise the heel" of God's people. (See Genesis 3:15.) The great tactic of the serpent is the infliction of pain and suffering.

• *Accuser of the Brethren.* This is the one who came before God's throne to argue against man's righteousness—including man's attitudes, thoughts, words, and deeds—just as satan accused Job of serving God only because he had been blessed by God (Job 2:1–10). The great tactic of the accuser is the destruction of a person's integrity or reputation.

The book of Revelation makes it clear that satan only functions within parameters *allowed* by God. He has access to the mind of mankind as part of God's gift of free will that allows a person to chose or reject God. In heaven mankind's free will will have been fully exercised—those who have chosen God will reap the rewards of heaven, those who have rejected God will be subjected to satan's punishment.

Revelation also affirms what is stated throughout the New Testament: the devil can be *deflected*, even if not fully defeated, by mankind. He can be resisted and made to flee (James 4:7). He can be cast out of those he possesses and cast away from those he oppresses (Matt. 10:1). He can be overcome (Rev. 2:11) by those who accept the salvation made possible by the shed blood of Jesus, who use the Word of God as a weapon against the devil, and who refuse to compromise with him regardless of the persecution brought against them.

The good news in Revelation is that the devil will have no more ability to pressure us to perform perfectly apart from God's help. His lies and temptations will end and so will his ability to cause pain and suffering. He can no longer destroy our integrity or reputation. He holds no power of fear. Rejoice. His demise is certain.

How has the enemy of your soul come against you? What are the foremost tactics he has used in your life?

How have *you* come against the enemy of your soul?

A
Application for Today

The young woman stared in amazement, seeing meaning in the object in front of her that no one else in her tour group seemed to see. She was standing in the emperor's throne room in the Forbidden City of Beijing. Her guide had just informed the group that the "chair" they were viewing was the ancient Chinese emperor's throne. It was made entirely of intertwined solid-gold serpents. The canopy over the throne had pillars that depicted solid-gold dragons spiraling their way up the vertical poles.

The guide casually explained that the unseen power of the emperor was perceived by the Chinese people to be given to the emperor by the Great Dragon, the largest and most powerful of all the dragons. It was believed that the dragon's spiritual power channeled directly *through* the emperor, allowing the emperor to exert absolute control over his subjects. The principal tactic was fear.

Furthermore, the guide explained, any place where one saw the image of a dragon in China, one should conclude that this was a place where the emperor was fully in control and the power of the dragon was held in highest esteem. The guide then said, perhaps trying to connect with his American tourists, "It is like a cross on a church symbolizing that Jesus is in control of the church. The sign of the dragon symbolized that the dragon was in control of the building."

The young woman sighed and said to her traveling companion, "I will never again regard a dragon at a Chinese restaurant as a piece of artwork or as an item of décor."

Do symbols embody meaning, even if those who see the symbol don't recognize that meaning? Why do we need to be cautious in our use of symbols? In what ways do we need to be cautious in our use of objects that have been created by pagan people?

Throughout church history, crosses have been carried into evil areas to convey a message of Christ's supremacy over the demons worshiped in that area. People have worn crosses to symbolize their belief in Jesus as Savior. Is the cross still a symbol of Christ's presence?

In what ways do symbols, for good or evil, infiltrate our thinking and become part of our mindsets, perspectives, and worldviews?

S
Supplementary Scriptures to Consider

While the vast majority of the book of Revelation appears to deal with future reality, the vision we discussed at the opening of this chapter apparently presents something that happened in ages past:

> And war broke out in heaven: Michael and his angels fought
> with the dragon; and the dragon and his angels fought, but
> they did not prevail, nor was a place found for them in heaven
> any longer. So the great dragon was cast out, that serpent of
> old, called the Devil and Satan, who deceives the whole
> world; he was cast to the earth, and his angels were cast out
> with him (Rev. 12:7–10).

• The good news is that the dragon and his angels did not prevail against Michael and his angels. Do you feel fully assured that nothing the devil does against you can prevail against the power of God?

• Given our discussion above about the terms ascribed to the devil, cite specific ways in which you may have experienced the devil functioning in these roles:

   satan (pressure of human perfection):

Devil (liar, deceiver, tempter):

Dragon (fear):

Serpent (pain and suffering):

Accuser (attacker of integrity, reputation):

John also had this vision about the demise of the devil and those who are in his camp:

> Then I saw an angel coming down from heaven, having the key to the bottomless pit and a great chain in his hand. He laid hold of the dragon, that serpent of old, who is the Devil and Satan, and bound him for a thousand years; and he cast him into the bottomless pit, and shut him up, and set a seal on him, so that he should deceive the nations no more till the thousand years were finished. But after these things he must be released for a little while . . .
>
> Now when the thousand years have expired, Satan will be released from his prison and will go out to deceive the nations which are in the four corners of the earth, Gog and Magog, to gather them together to battle, whose number is as the sand of the sea. They went up on the breadth of the earth and sur-rounded the camp of the saints and the beloved city. And fire came down from God out of heaven and devoured them. The devil, who deceived them, was cast into the lake of fire and

brimstone where the beast and the false prophet are. And they will be tormented day and night forever and ever (Rev. 20:1–3, 7–10).

• What can you conclude with certainty from this passage? Who is in control of what happens to the devil?

John had this vision about what Jesus will do in judgment of the nations:

Now I saw heaven opened, and behold, a white horse. And he who sat on him was called Faithful and True, and in righteousness He judges and makes war. His eyes were like a flame of fire, and on His head were many crowns. He had a name written that no one knew except Himself. He was clothed with a robe dipped in blood, and His name is called the Word of God. And the armies in heaven, clothed in fine linen, white and clean, followed Him on white horses. Now out of His mouth goes a sharp sword, that with it He should strike the nations. And He Himself will rule them with a rod of iron. He Himself treads the winepress of the fierceness and wrath of Almighty God. And He has on His robe and on His thigh a name written:

KING OF KINGS

AND LORD OF LORDS.

Then I saw an angel standing in the sun; and he cried with a loud voice, saying to all the birds that fly in the midst of heaven. "Come and gather together for the supper of the great God, that you may eat the flesh of kings, the flesh of captains, the flesh of mighty men, the flesh of horses and of those who sit on them, and the flesh of all people, free and slave, both small and great."

And I saw the beast, the kings of the earth, and their armies, gathered together to make war against Him who sat on the horse and against His army. Then the beast was captured, and with him the false prophet who worked signs in his presence, by which he deceived those who received the mark of the beast and those who worshiped his image. These two were cast alive into the lake of fire burning with brimstone. And the rest were killed with the sword which proceeded from the mouth of Him who sat on the horse. And all the birds were filled with their flesh (Rev. 19:11–21).

- What does this passage say will happen to those nations that have aligned with the devil to inflict evil on God's people?

John had this vision about the final judgment of all people:

Then I saw a great white throne and Him who sat on it, from whose face the earth and the heaven fled away. And there was found no place for them. And I saw the dead, small and great, standing before God, and books were opened. And another book was opened, which is the Book of Life. And the dead were judged according to their works, by the things which were written in the books. The sea gave up the dead who were in it, and Death and Hades delivered up the dead who were in them. And they were judged, each one according to his works. Then Death and Hades were cast into the lake of fire. This is the second death. And anyone not found written the Book of Life was cast into the lake of fire (Rev. 20:11–15).

- What does this passage tells us about the final judgment all people will one day face?

- The Jews and early Christians had a very strong understanding that believing and receiving Christ fell into a category of works of faith (versus works of effort). How does knowing that impact your interpretation of this passage?

- This passage tells us that *Death* will be cast into the lake of fire; it will be eliminated. How does this influence your understanding of what it means, as a believer in Christ Jesus, to have the promise of everlasting life?

I
Introspection and Implications

1. Do you consider yourself to be victorious over the enemy of your soul? How so? In what ways? With what limitations?

2. Does knowing more about the nature—the identity and characteristics—of the enemy of your soul help you in battling him? How so?

3. Many people seem to attribute the bad things that happen in their life as being something God did to them. What would John say about that? What is the danger of attributing to God what should actually be attributed to the devil?

Communicating the Good News

To what extent should we include the good news that Jesus is triumphant over satan as part of our evangelistic messages?

LESSON #7

OUR HEAVENLY HOME

Heaven: the eternal home of all Christians, who will dwell there with God the Father, Christ Jesus, and the host of creatures and angels created by God

B
Bible Focus

> Now I saw a new heaven and a new earth, for the first
> heaven and the first earth had passed away. Also there was no
> more sea. Then I, John, saw the holy city, New Jerusalem,
> coming down out of heaven from God, prepared as a bride
> adorned for her husband. And I heard a loud voice from
> heaven saying, "Behold, the tabernacle of God is with men,
> and He will dwell with them, and they shall be His people.
> God Himself will be with them and be their God. And God will
> wipe away every tear from their eyes; there shall be no more
> death, nor sorrow, nor crying. There shall be no more pain,
> for the former things have passed away."
>
> Then He who sat on the throne said, "Behold, I make all
> things new." And He said to me, "Write, for these words are
> true and faithful."
>
> And He said to me, "It is done. I am the Alpha and the
> Omega, the Beginning and the End. I will give of the fountain
> of the water of life freely to him who thirsts. He who over-
> comes shall inherit all things, and I will be his God and he
> shall be My son. But the cowardly, unbelieving, abominable,
> murderers, sexually immoral, sorcerers, idolaters, and all liars
> shall have their part in the lake which burns with fire and
> brimstone, which is the second death" (Rev. 21:1–8).

John had a vision in which *all* things became new. That is something few
people have ever fully contemplated; it is impossible for the human mind to
fully understand how all things that are presently known become new. In
some cases, the newness might be a new design never before encountered by
human senses. In other cases, the newness might be a full restoration to the
perfection of Eden, a perfection no person has ever experienced and cannot
fully fathom. Perhaps other newness will involve the completion or fulfill-
ment of things only partially experienced in our humanity. Whatever form
newness takes, it is the creative work of Almighty God.

For the believer, the new heaven and earth are a place of bliss. This
passage from Revelation affirms, like other passages in the book, that the
new heaven and earth are the domain of those who have overcome the devil
and are God's beloved children. Those who have lived evil lives, without
turning to God in sorrow and repentance to receive His forgiveness, will not
experience the new heaven and the new earth.

Note that the Lord said this about the new world He would be creating:

• *God is fully united with His people.* There is no greater hope than this: that we will dwell forever in the near presence of God. He will dwell with us and we with Him. We will fully assume our identity as God's people, and nothing we do or fail to do will have any impact upon God's presence with us.

This was an especially powerful reaffirmation to the Jews who heard the words of this vision read in their midst. They knew that God had said this about the Israelites, "They will be my people and I will be their God" (Lev. 26:12, Jer. 11:4). The Jews also knew that their ancestors had fluctuated in their obedience to God and, as a consequence, had experienced a fluctuation in the blessings they received from God. At last, in our new eternal home, all who are the people of God will obey God fully, trust in God fully, and receive the fullness of all God has prepared for them. There will no longer be even the hint of an inclination in any human heart to do *anything* contrary to God's command. We at last will be in complete harmony with God our Creator.

• *God will wipe every tear from all eyes. There will be no more death, sorrow, or crying. There will be no more pain.* In the new heaven and earth, every person is in total obedience to God's will, and all creation will be in harmony. Disobedience brought about the Fall in the Garden of Eden. The result was death, sorrow, and pain. In the new heaven and earth, disobedience is not an option. The heart and mind of each resident of the new creation will have made a choice for lasting obedience. That decision will be sealed for eternity. John recorded these words, "The former things have passed away." All of the systems and protocols man generated in order to justify sin, accommodate death, attempt to ease pain and sorrow, and avoid judgment will pass away. They no longer will have any use.

• *God will give a fountain of water of life freely to him who thirsts.* Everything we know as the goodness of life, the abundant, refreshing, fulfilling aspects of life, will overflow and be freely given in this new heaven and earth. Any person who has even the slightest desire (thirst) for anything that is life-giving will have that desire more than satisfied. Few people today can claim to have experienced even a short period of total abundance in all areas of their lives, simultaneously—spiritually, physically, emotionally, mentally, relationally, and materially. A life of total abundance will forever be ours.

• *God will cause those who have been faithful to Him to inherit all things.*
We will have total access to all that is God's.

Ultimately, the new heaven and new earth will be full of the presence of
God and His people, a place *without sin*. We can hardly imagine it. But we
can trust that it *will happen*. And we are wise to prepare for it. God made it
equally clear through this vision that there are those who will *not* experience
the new heaven and new earth. The decision about who enters the new
heaven and new earth, and who has part in the lake that burns with fire and
brimstone, is a decision man makes and God only confirms against the
absolute commands of His Word.

Note these words of Jesus, "It is done." John, the apostle, stood at the foot
of the cross of Calvary and was very likely present when Jesus cried, "It is
finished," as He exhaled His dying breath. Jesus had accomplished all that
was necessary for God's reconciliation with mankind.

Here, Jesus says, "It is finished," to signify that what He did at the outset
of Creation will be fully restored. The plan of God will have come full
circle. What *was* perfect will be perfect again.

How glorious that will be—beyond anything we can fathom.

A
Application for Today

A young couple had chosen a fairly uncommon place for their honey-
moon: Lapland. They had traveled to this area near the Arctic Circle in hopes
of experiencing something both of them had long desired to see: the North-
ern Lights. They had not been disappointed. For several nights they sat for
long hours experiencing what they now called "God's Ultimate Light Show."

"What was it really like?" a friend asked.

The bride said, "We have tried very hard to come up with the right words,
and we think this is one of those experiences that can't be captured in words.
It was amazing, awesome, life-changing, powerful, inspiring, creative,
spiritual, dramatic—but it was so much *more* than that. Those words only
barely touch the surface of what we saw and felt."

The groom added, "Do you know that old gospel song that talks about
something being a 'foretaste of glory divine'?" The friend nodded "yes."

"Well, it was a foretaste of glory divine," he said. "And, if anything, this
experience changed our concept of heaven, too. If God could give us such an
awesome display here on earth, there is simply no imagining what awaits us
in eternity."

As you think about heaven, what adjectives or other words do you use to
describe heaven? In what ways do you suspect those words are inadequate?

S
Supplementary Scriptures to Consider

John had a vision of the church, the bride of Christ, as being one and the same as the New Jerusalem:

> Then one of the seven angels who had the seven bowls filled with the seven last plagues came to me and talked with me, saying, "Come, I will show you the bride, the Lamb's wife." And he carried me away in the Spirit to a great and high mountain, and showed me the great city, the holy Jerusalem, descending out of heaven from God, having the glory of God. Her light was like a most precious stone, like a jasper stone, clear as crystal. Also she had a great and high wall with twelve gates, and twelve angels at the gates, and names written on them, which are the names of the twelve tribes of the children of Israel: three gates on the east, three gates on the north, three gates on the south, and three gates on the west.
>
> Now the wall of the city had twelve foundations, and on them were the names of the twelve apostles of the Lamb. And he who talked with me had a gold reed to measure the city, its gates, and its wall. The city is laid out as a square; its length is as great as its breadth. And he measured the city with the reed: twelve thousand furlongs. Its length, breadth, and height are equal. Then he measured its wall: one hundred and forty-four cubits, according to the measure of a man, that is, of an angel. The construction of its wall was of jasper; and the city was pure gold, like clear glass. The foundations of the wall of the city were adorned with all kinds of precious stones: the first foundation was jasper, the second sapphire, the third chalcedony, the fourth emerald, the fifth sardonyx, the sixth sardius, the seventh chrysolite, the eighth beryl, the ninth topaz, the tenth chrysoprase, the eleventh jacinth, and the twelfth amethyst. The twelve gates were twelve pearls: each individual gate was of one pearl. And the street of the city was pure gold, like transparent glass (Rev. 21:9–21).

• What is it about this description of the New Jerusalem that produces great excitement in you?

John had this insight into what he did *not* see in heaven:

> But I saw no temple in it, for the Lord God Almighty and the Lamb are its temple. The city had no need of the sun or of the moon to shine in it, for the glory of God illuminated it. The Lamb is its light. And the nations of those who are saved shall walk in its light, and the kings of the earth bring their glory and honor into it. Its gates shall not be shut at all by day (there shall be no night there). And they shall bring the glory and the honor of the nations into it. But there shall by no means enter it anything that defiles, or causes an abomination or a lie, but only those who are written in the Lamb's Book of Life (Rev. 21:22–27).

• Every culture and every religion on earth, throughout history, has constructed shrines or buildings to house God. There is no need for a place to house God because all of heaven is housed *in* God. How does this relate to your understanding of what it means to be *in Christ* as a believer on the earth today?

John had this vision of our eternal home:

> And he showed me a pure river of water of life, clear as crystal, proceeding from the throne of God and of the Lamb. In the middle of its street, and on either side of the river, was the tree of life, which bore twelve fruits, each tree yielding its fruit every month. The leaves of the tree were for the healing of the nations. And there shall be no more curse, but the throne of God and of the Lamb shall be in it, and His servants shall serve Him. They shall see His face, and His name shall be on their foreheads. There shall be no night there: They need

no lamp nor light of the sun, for the Lord God gives them light. And they shall reign forever and ever (Rev. 22:1–5).

• Does life flow from God to you today? How so?

• In what ways does God provide healing for His people today?

• Respond to the statement: "They shall see His face and His name shall be on their foreheads."

I
Introspection and Implications

1. What are you most looking forward to experiencing in heaven?

2. Do you believe heaven will be exciting or boring? Do you believe it will be a place of ongoing activity and challenge?

3. Why do you believe what you believe about heaven?

4. In what ways must we trust God to bring about all that we hope regarding eternity and heaven?

C
Communicating the Good News

"Everybody will eventually get to heaven. God wouldn't send anybody to hell—not if He is a truly loving God." What would you say to a person who voiced these statements to you? Why? Using what evidence for your response?

How important is it that our evangelistic messages present the hope of heaven and an eternity spent in the near presence of God? In what ways can we present that hope?

NOTES TO LEADERS
OF SMALL GROUPS

As the leader of a small discussion group, think of yourself as a facilitator with three main roles:

- Get the discussion started.

- Involve every person in the group.

- Encourage an open, candid discussion that remains Bible-focused.

You certainly don't need to be the person with all the answers! In truth, much of your role is to be a person who asks questions:

- What really impacted you most in this lesson?

- Was there a particular part of the lesson or a question that you found troubling?

- Was there a particular part of the lesson that you found encouraging or insightful?

- Was there a particular part of the lesson that you'd like to explore further?

Express to the group at the outset of your study that your goal as a group is to gain new insights into God's Word; this is not the forum for defending a point of doctrine or a theological opinion. Stay focused on what God's Word says and means. The purpose of the study is also to share insights on how to apply God's Word to everyday life. *Every* person in the group can and should contribute. The collective wisdom that flows from Bible-focused discussion is often very rich and deep.

Seek to create an environment in which every member of the group feels free to ask questions of other members in order to gain greater understanding. Encourage the group members to voice their appreciation to one another for new insights gained and be supportive of one another. Take the lead in this. Genuinely appreciate and value the contributions made by each person.

Since the letters of Paul are geared to our personal Christian lives as well as to the life of the church as a whole, you may experience a tendency in your group sessions to become overly critical of your *own* church or church leaders. Avoid the tendency to create discord or dissatisfaction. Don't use this Bible study as an opportunity to spread rumor, air anyone's dirty laundry, or criticize your pastor. Rather, seek positive ways to build up one another, including your church leaders. Seek positive outcomes and solutions to any problems you may identify.

You may want to begin each study by having one or more members of the group read through the section provided under "Bible Focus." Ask the group specifically if it desires to discuss any of the questions under the "Application" section, the "Supplemental Scriptures" section, and the "Implications" and "Communicating the Gospel" sections. You do not need to bring closure—or come to a definitive conclusion or consensus—about any one question asked in this study. Rather, if the group does not *have* a satisfactory Bible-based answer , encourage them to engage in further "asking, seeking, and knocking" strategies to discover the answers! Remember the words of Jesus: "Ask, and it will be given to you, seek, and you will find; knock, and it will be opened to you. For everyone who asks receives, and he who seeks finds, and to him who knocks it will be opened" (Matt. 7:7–8).

Finally, open and close your study with prayer. Ask the Holy Spirit, whom Jesus called the Spirit of Truth, to guide your discussion and to reveal what is of eternal benefit to you individually and as a group. As you close your study, ask the Holy Spirit to seal to your remembrance what you have read and studied and to show you in the upcoming days, weeks, and months *ways* to apply what you have studied to your daily life and relationships.

General Themes for the Lessons

Each lesson in this study has one or more core themes. Continually pull the group back to these themes. You can do this by asking simple questions, such as, "How does that relate to _____?" or "How does that help us better understand the concept of _____?" or "In what ways does that help us apply the principle of _____?"

A summary of general themes or concepts in each lesson is provided below:

Lesson #1
CHRIST IN THE MIDST OF HIS CHURCH
Growing in our understanding of Jesus—who He was on earth and who He is in heaven

God is in control of all things at all times

The confidence gained by an awareness of Christ's presence: that we are held by Him and He is in our midst

Lesson #2
COUNSEL TO THE CHURCHES IN EPHESUS AND PARGAMOS
Repentance

Reaffirmation of one's first love, Jesus

Refusing to compromise with the world

Having ears to hear what the Spirit says

Being an overcomer

Lesson #3
COUNSEL TO THE CHURCHES OF THYATIRA, SARDIS, AND LAODICEA
Compromising with the world—our distinctiveness as Christians

The hallmarks of spiritual *life*

Taking a stand for the Lord

Lesson #4
AFFIRMATION OF THE CHURCHES IN SMYRNA AND PHILADELPHIA
Courage in the face of persecution

God-given opportunities

Enhanced witness in the face of difficulties

Lesson #5
PRAISE IN THE THRONE ROOM OF HEAVEN
The role of praise as part of a person's spiritual life and growth

These attributes of God: holiness, omnipotence, everlastingness

Lesson #6

VICTORY OVER SATAN AND ALL GOD'S ENEMIES

The nature and tactics of our enemy and the degree we should be concerned about him

Confronting the enemy of our souls

Lesson #7

OUR HEAVENLY HOME

The new heaven and new earth

The residents of heaven

NOTES

NOTES

NOTES

NOTES

NOTES

NOTES

CPSIA information can be obtained at www.ICGtesting.com
Printed in the USA
LVOW060735250911

247719LV00006B/4/P